SOCIAL STUDIES EXPLORER

It's Cool to Learn About America's Waterways

PUGET SOUND

➠ by Katie Marsico

CHERRY LAKE PUBLISHING • ANN ARBOR, MICHIGAN

Published in the United States of America
by Cherry Lake Publishing
Ann Arbor, Michigan
www.cherrylakepublishing.com

Content Adviser: James Wolfinger, PhD, Associate Professor,
History and Teacher Education, DePaul University, Chicago, Illinois

Book Design: The Design Lab

Photo Credits: Cover and page 3, ©iStockphoto.com/jcarillet, ©Bill Perry/
Shutterstock, Inc., ©Norma Cornes/Shutterstock, Inc., ©63957112/
Shutterstock, Inc., ©AlexanderZam/Shutterstock, Inc.; back cover and
page 3, ©Natalia Bratslavsky/Shutterstock, Inc.; page 4, ©Stacey Lynn
Payne/Shutterstock, Inc.; page 5, ©Mark Payne/Shutterstock, Inc.; page
6, ©Videowokart/Shutterstock, Inc.; page 8, ©Wend Images/Alamy;
pages 9 and 11, ©Danita Delimon/Alamy; page 10, ©UgputuLf SS/
Shutterstock, Inc.; page 12, ©Adrian Baras/Shutterstock, Inc.; page 14,
©Jeff Rotman/Alamy; page 15, ©Matt Ragen/Shutterstock, Inc.; page
16, © 2009fotofriends/Shutterstock, Inc.; page 18, ©North Wind Picture
Archives/Alamy; page 19, ©kwest/Shutterstock, Inc.; page 21, ©Vivian
Mcaleavey/Dreamstime.com; page 22, ©VanHart/Shutterstock, Inc.; page
23, ©iPixela/Shutterstock, Inc.; page 26, ©Mark Payne/Shutterstock, Inc.,
page 28, ©Murray Landauer/Shutterstock, Inc.

Library of Congress Cataloging-in-Publication Data
Marsico, Katie, 1980–
    Puget Sound / by Katie Marsico.
        p. cm. — (It's cool to learn about America's waterways)
    Includes bibliographical references and index.
    ISBN 978-1-62431-015-7 (lib. bdg.) — ISBN 978-1-62431-039-3 (pbk.)
— ISBN 978-1-62431-063-8 (e-book)
 1. Puget Sound (Wash.)—Juvenile literature I. Title.
 F897.P9M37 2013
 551.46'1432—dc23   2012034741

Cherry Lake Publishing would like to acknowledge the work
of The Partnership for 21st Century Skills. Please visit
www.21stcenturyskills.org for more information.

Printed in the United States of America
Corporate Graphics Inc.
January 2013
CLSP12

PUGET SOUND

TABLE OF CONTENTS

CHAPTER ONE

WELCOME TO PUGET SOUND!

→ Ferries allow people to travel quickly between the many towns and cities located along Puget Sound.

Are you excited about exploring Puget Sound? This **estuary** is located in northwestern Washington State. It is an inlet, or arm, of the Pacific Ocean. As you travel around Puget Sound, you'll observe an amazing variety of wildlife, including sea otters, salmon, and the largest octopuses in the world. You'll ride a passenger boat called a ferry and get splashed during a whale-watching tour. You'll also learn about local culture and **cuisine**. And if you've never tried **shellfish** before, you'll have the chance to sample some delicious recipes! Yet your journey will involve much more than tasty food and fun tourist attractions. You will also discover what part you can play in protecting this incredible American waterway from pollution and other threats.

You're probably eager to get going. But it's important that you properly prepare for your trip. For starters, you need to know exactly where you're headed. Puget Sound is not far from the border that separates the United States from Canada. This waterway measures 2,800 square miles (7,252 square kilometers). Its average depth is 430 to 450 feet (131 to 137 meters). The entire sound features approximately 2,500 miles (4,023 km) of U.S. shoreline.

Want to learn a little more about this waterway's geography? Puget Sound is made up of deep basins and sills. A basin is a sunken area in the earth's surface that is often filled with water. A sill is an underwater ridge that separates two side-by-side basins. These formations divide Puget Sound into five regions. They are North Puget Sound, Main Basin, Whidbey Basin, South Puget Sound, and Hood Canal.

●➤ The Cascades lie to the east and south of Puget Sound.

Roughly 10,000 tributaries flow into Puget Sound. A tributary is a river or stream that empties into a larger body of water. The sound's major tributaries include the Nooksack, Samish, Skagit, Stillaguamish, and Snohomish Rivers. The Puget Sound region lies between Washington's Cascade and Olympic Mountains. It features 19 major watersheds. A watershed is the area drained by a waterway and all of its tributaries.

Water in Puget Sound is a mix of freshwater and saltwater. Melting snow in nearby mountain ranges feeds the thousands of streams and rivers that provide Puget Sound with freshwater. The sound receives most of its saltwater from the **Strait** of Juan de Fuca, which is Puget Sound's connection to the Pacific Ocean. Portions of the sound are also filled with brackish water, a blend of freshwater and saltwater. Puget Sound, the Strait of Juan de Fuca, and the Strait of Georgia are part of a larger body of water known as the Salish Sea.

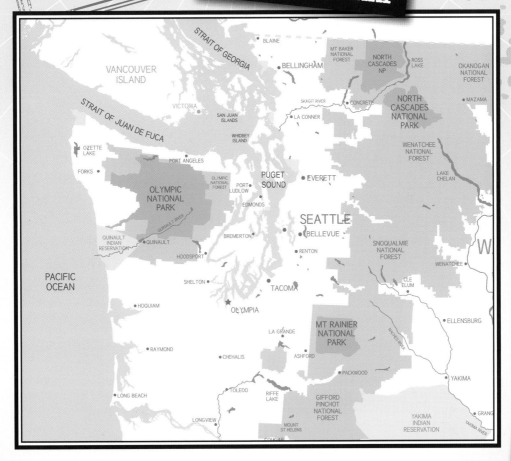

Carefully review this map of Puget Sound. Then lay a separate piece of paper over it and trace the waterway's outline. Use a crayon or marker to shade in the Puget Sound region. Also label the Pacific Ocean and the Salish Sea (including the Strait of Juan de Fuca and Strait of Georgia). Draw small triangles to mark where the Cascade and Olympic Mountains are as well. Feel free to add any other important locations you discover as you continue your adventure!

STOP
Don't write in this book!

● Gravel covers a large portion of Puget Sound's coastline.

Before you tour Puget Sound, you should know that you're going to be a busy traveler! This is because the local **ecosystem** includes a wide variety of **habitats**. Rivers and **mudflats** are just two examples of the natural environments you'll explore in the Puget Sound region. Other habitats you'll discover include rocky shores and eelgrass beds. Eelgrass beds are thick patches of underwater grass.

Puget Sound also features salt marshes, or low-lying grasslands that are regularly flooded by saltwater. Some parts of the sound are bordered by gravel beaches. If you plan on

strolling along one of them, consider packing a pair of flip-flops. Because gravel is a loose mixture of sand and small rocks, going barefoot might be a bit bumpy!

Of course, you should bring a pair of walking shoes, too. They'll come in handy if you decide to hike across any of the **bluffs** bordering Puget Sound. These steep banks slope toward the water and form another part of the local ecosystem. Now, start thinking about the weather in the Puget Sound region. Then you can figure out what else to pack!

◆ Some bluffs overlooking Puget Sound are extremely steep.

Be sure to find a spot in your suitcase for your umbrella and raincoat. The Puget Sound region—like much of Washington State—is famous for its rainfall. You have less chance of getting soaked if you visit in summer, because fall, winter, and spring are the sound's rainiest seasons. Winter snow is common, especially if you're traveling closer to the mountains. Snow and rain are examples of precipitation, or moisture that falls to the earth's surface. Yearly precipitation totals for much of the Puget Sound region measure between 19 and 56 inches (48 and 142 centimeters).

↔ Rainstorms are common in the Puget Sound area.

➤ Snow sometimes blankets the Puget Sound region during winter.

If you're heading to the area in winter, pack your hat and gloves. Depending on which part of the sound you're touring, January temperatures generally range from 33 degrees Fahrenheit (0.6 degrees Celsius) to 49°F (9.4°C). Meanwhile, you can probably get away with bringing just a light sweater in July, when average temperatures are usually between 51°F and 78°F (10.6°C and 25.6°C).

Do you plan on swimming in Puget Sound? If so, tuck your swimsuit or trunks somewhere inside your suitcase—and prepare to do a few bobs to get used to the chilly waves! Average water temperatures are typically between 44°F and 56°F (6.7°C and 13.3°C). When you're done choosing what clothes to take on your Puget Sound adventure, start packing the equipment you'll need for some serious wildlife watching!

CHAPTER TWO

THE WATERWAY'S WILDLIFE

↪ Maples found in the Puget Sound region turn beautiful shades of orange, red, and yellow in fall.

It's a good idea to have a camera when you explore Puget Sound. Practice using it, too. This way, you'll be ready to snap scenic photos of the incredible plant life in and along the waterway. Both big-leaf and vine maples are found throughout the Puget Sound region. Evergreens such as shore pines, Sitka spruce, madrones, and Pacific yews grow there as well. If you look high above you, you might see western red cedars towering more than 200 feet (61 m) high. Aim your camera toward the ground to photograph shrubs. Oregon grapes,

snowberries, wild roses, and red and evergreen huckleberries are all common in the region.

Want to take a peek at Puget Sound's underwater plants? Pack your swim goggles and keep your eyes peeled for meadows of eelgrass. This underwater grass shouldn't be too hard to spot. That is because its blades, or leaves, often measure almost 3 feet (0.9 m) long! You can also use your goggles to study the several different types of kelp that float throughout the sound. Twenty-six species of this large brown seaweed exist within the waterway.

The plant life you'll see in Puget Sound plays an important part in the local ecosystem. The roots of various trees and shrubs that grow in the Puget Sound region form a type of underground web. The roots anchor the soil in place and help prevent wind and water from wearing it away. In many cases, plants ranging from eelgrass to evergreens also provide food and shelter to the thousands of animals that depend on the sound for survival.

Have you ever heard of a geoduck? This animal isn't actually a duck. It's a giant clam that burrows deep into the sandy mud in Puget Sound. Geoducks are one of the more than 3,000 species of **mollusks**, sea urchins, starfish, and crabs found in the waterway. The world's largest octopus also lives in the sound. Known as the North Pacific giant octopus, it can stretch up to 30 feet (9.1 m) long. It might weigh as much as 125 pounds (57 kilograms)! This octopus shares Puget Sound with more than 300 species of fish. Chinook salmon and six-gilled sharks are just two examples. The sound is also home to steelhead, herring, cod, dogfish, and rockfish.

➡ The North Pacific giant octopus uses its long arms to grab nearby prey.

•◦ Visitors often travel to Puget Sound in hopes of sighting orcas.

Pack a pair of binoculars if you want to stand along the shore and search the waves for dolphins and porpoises. These marine mammals are often visible when they come to the surface of the water to breathe air. Seals, sea lions, and otters spend time in Puget Sound as well.

Chances are good that you've already heard about the waterway's whale population. In fact, people often think of killer whales—or orcas—as a symbol of Puget Sound. If you're lucky, you might spot minke whales, gray whales, and humpback whales, too!

➥ Black bears are among the largest land animals found in the Puget Sound region.

You can use your binoculars to do a little bird-watching, too. See if you can spy a tufted puffin or bufflehead! Sandpipers, herons, loons, and diving ducks called scoters are also found along the sound. If you pay close attention, you might even glimpse a bald eagle flying overhead!

You don't necessarily have to look toward the sky or the water to see Puget Sound wildlife. For example, black-tailed deer, black bears, cougars, coyotes, and cottontail rabbits roam the region's many bluffs. If you hope to catch a glimpse of these and the thousands of other animals that make up the local ecosystem, hurry up and finish packing! Once you do, you'll have to take a little side trip before you officially start your journey around Puget Sound.

Make Your Very Own Field Guide

How do you plan to keep track of all the different plants and animals that live in and near Puget Sound? Try using a field guide! This type of book features descriptions of the various species of wildlife that exist in a certain environment. Make your own field guide to stay organized during your adventure around the sound. Simply pick 20 species of local wildlife (or more if you want). Write the name of each one on a separate sheet of paper. Next, prepare to do a little detective work on the computer or at your local library. Track down and record the following information for all the plants and animals you have chosen:

Type of plant/animal: (tree, shrub, flower/
    reptile, mammal, fish)
Habitat:
Appearance:
Other interesting facts:

    Once you've done this, either print out or draw pictures of the species that you included. Lastly, decorate a cover and staple your pages together, or snap them into a binder. Most importantly, don't forget to bring your field guide along when you visit Puget Sound!

CHAPTER THREE

PAST AND PRESENT

☙ Europeans began settling what would become the northwestern United States during the 1800s.

As you head toward Puget Sound, pretend that you're not traveling to visit a remarkable American waterway. Instead, pretend you're going to a land of endless ice! This is what the Puget Sound region looked like 20,000 years ago. Back then, **glaciers** filled the space between the Cascade and Olympic Mountains. Over the next several thousand years, these huge glaciers would grind across the land and melt, shaping the surface and carving out what is now Puget Sound.

Early peoples probably began living in this area about 8,000 years ago. Several American Indian groups built villages in the

Puget Sound region. Many Native American groups continue to make up an important part of the population there. They include the Nooksack, Lummi, Swinomish, Stillaguamish, Tulalip, Suquamish, Nisqually, and Skokomish nations.

Europeans began exploring Puget Sound in the late 1700s. They quickly realized that it was a valuable source of fish and timber. In 1846, the waterway became a part of the United States.

Today, the Puget Sound region is home to approximately 4.3 million people. Roughly 37 percent of them live in the 90 towns and cities located directly on the sound. Major cities include Seattle, Tacoma, and Olympia. Fishing, shipping, tourism, **recreational** activities such as boating, and other local businesses add about $20 billion to the state **economy**.

•❖ Seattle is the largest city on Puget Sound.

ACTIVITY

TEST YOUR KNOWLEDGE

It's quiz time! Complete the matching activity below to test how much you know about the history of Puget Sound. On the left side, you'll see the names of five people who are connected to the waterway. On the right side, you'll see a description of the reasons these individuals are famous. Try to match each person with the correct description!

1) George Vancouver

2) Chief Seattle

3) George Washington Bush

4) Emma Smith DeVoe

5) Bill Gates

A) Duwamish leader who encouraged respect for the environment and who supported peaceful relations with white settlers in the Puget Sound region

B) African American who led the first group of U.S. citizens to settle along Puget Sound and develop successful farms in the area

C) Tacoma resident who was involved in state and national politics, including the fight to help women earn the right to vote

D) Founder of the computer software company Microsoft who was born in (and still lives in) the Puget Sound region

E) British explorer who journeyed along North America's Pacific Coast and named Puget Sound

STOP
Don't write in this book!

Answers: 1) E; 2) A; 3) B; 4) C; 5) D

Arrange a ferry ride with Puget Sound Express if you want to do a little whale-watching between Port Townsend and the San Juan Islands. Many guides guarantee that you'll spot orcas at some point during your cruise.

Head to Penrose Point State Park in Lakebay to observe wildlife on the beach and along the bluffs overlooking the sound. The park is also the perfect location for camping, hiking, and biking.

It's important to understand how American Indians have shaped Puget Sound's history and culture. Check out the Suquamish Museum at the Port Madison Indian Reservation and the Hibulb Cultural Center in Tulalip. There you can find out more about local Native Americans and their traditions.

➻ The San Juan Islands lie at the northern end of Puget Sound.

➥ The Space Needle is the most distinctive feature in the Seattle skyline.

As you near the end of your journey around Puget Sound, spend a few hours touring the Seattle area. A tower called the Space Needle is one of the sound's most famous attractions. Ride an elevator 520 feet (158 m) up to reach the observation deck. You'll experience the most amazing view of the water-way you just explored!

Once you get back on the ground, stop your sightseeing and silence your grumbling tummy. The Puget Sound region offers many delicious foods that are sure to make your mouth water. You'll find many restaurants located along the sound that feature salmon and shellfish dishes. If the weather is cold and wet, try a cup of steaming hot chowder to warm you up! Chowders are thick stews or soups that contain potatoes, onions, corn, and clams or fish. For dessert, dig into a piece of freshly baked berry pie. The juicy berries in its filling were most likely grown on local farms.

After you finish chowing down, take one last relaxing stroll along the shore. Then start packing to go home. Don't say good-bye to the waterway just yet, though. Instead, finish off your adventure by focusing on what you can do to care for the national treasure known as Puget Sound.

⊷ There are many different recipes for chowder. This creamy chowder includes clams.

Shellfish is a big part of Puget Sound cuisine, but perhaps a plate of raw clams isn't your thing. Don't worry. Just get creative and come up with a recipe that lets you sample a new food while still making your taste buds tingle! For example, try shellfish by making tasty Puget Sound clam rolls. Be sure to have an adult help you operate the oven and do the cutting for you.

Puget Sound Clam Rolls

INGREDIENTS

Cooking spray
1 small onion
2 10-ounce cans minced clams
2 cups flour
4 teaspoons baking powder
1½ teaspoons salt
½ cup shortening
¾ cup milk
1 tablespoon bread crumbs
1 cup grated cheese
1 cup tomato soup

INSTRUCTIONS

1. Preheat the oven to 400°F (204°C) and lightly coat a baking sheet with cooking spray.

2. Peel the onion and dice it into very small pieces. Set aside in a separate bowl.

3. Drain the cans of minced clams in a strainer over the sink. Set aside.

4. Mix the flour, baking powder, and ½ teaspoon of the salt in a bowl. Then add the shortening and milk. Stir these ingredients together until they form a dough.

5. Sprinkle a few pinches of flour onto a clean surface, where you can shape your dough into a flattened loaf. The loaf should be about ¼ inch (0.6 cm) thick.

6. Stir the clams, bread crumbs, cheese, and the remaining 1 teaspoon salt into the bowl containing the diced onion. Add a few spoonfuls of the soup to keep your mixture moist.

7. Spread the clam mixture onto your dough. Roll the dough into the shape of a log and then slice it into 6 pieces that are each about 1 ½ inches (4 cm) thick.

8. Carefully move the clam rolls onto the greased baking sheet. Place it in the oven and bake for 30 minutes. Let the rolls cool before enjoying a unique shellfish biscuit that is sure to remind you of Puget Sound!

CHAPTER FOUR

TAKING CARE OF A NATIONAL TREASURE

⇢ Pollution caused by human activities is damaging habitats in the Puget Sound region.

Puget Sound faces several serious threats. The chemicals that are present in **runoff** pollute the environment and ruin the land and water that many plants and animals need to survive.

Scientists estimate that, over the past 125 years, 70 percent of the sound's natural habitats have been damaged or have completely disappeared. As a result, several plant and animal species that live in the Puget Sound region are at risk of being completely wiped off the earth.

ACTIVITY

The killer whales living in Puget Sound are an example of the waterway's endangered wildlife. Scientists have been studying these orcas for many years. In 1974, scientists noted that the sound served as a year-round home for roughly 70 killer whales. By 1995, the local orca population had climbed to 98. Then in 2001, the number dropped to 81. As of 2011, scientists counted 88 killer whales in the sound. They hope to find at least 95 orcas living there in 2020.

Create a line graph based on the information you've just read. Use dots to show the killer whale population in Puget Sound in 1974, 1995, 2001, and 2011. Also include a dot for the number that scientists would like to see in 2020. When you connect the dots with a line, what does the graph tell you about the sound's changing orca population?

STOP
Don't write in
this book!

Population of Orcas

100

50

0

1974   1995   2001   2011   2020

Scientists, government leaders, and average U.S. citizens are all joining together to encourage **conservation** in the Puget Sound region. Some of their efforts involve closely studying the water. Conservationists pay careful attention to the chemicals that are present in the sound and how they're getting there. In other cases, people clean up and restore polluted habitats.

A huge part of conservation has to do with education. That is where you come in! Talk to your family and friends about what you have learned during your adventure around Puget Sound. Discuss the sound's incredible ecosystem and fascinating history. Share why everyone should be responsible for the survival of this remarkable American waterway.

➻ Help spread the word about the natural beauty and incredible history of Puget Sound.

Politicians in Washington State have the power to help protect Puget Sound. Along with political leaders across the rest of the nation, they vote on laws and government projects that impact America's waterways. Writing a letter to these men and women lets them know that you care about the sound. Ask an adult to help you find the addresses of officials who are trying to encourage conservation efforts. Then create a short, simple letter using the following outline:

Dear [INSERT THE NAME OF THE POLITICIAN(S) YOU DECIDE TO WRITE TO]:

I am writing to ask for your help in protecting Puget Sound. The sound is important to me because [INSERT TWO OR THREE REASONS THE SOUND MATTERS TO YOU].

Thanks for your efforts to support this amazing American waterway!

Sincerely,

[INSERT YOUR NAME]

STOP
Don't write in this book!

GLOSSARY

bluffs (BLUHFS) steep cliffs

conservation (kahn-sur-VAY-shuhn) the protection of valuable things, especially wildlife, natural resources, forests, or artistic or historic objects

cuisine (kwi-ZEEN) a style or manner of cooking or presenting food

economy (i-KAH-nuh-mee) the system of buying, selling, making things, and managing money in a place

ecosystem (EE-koh-sis-tuhm) all the livings things in a place and their relation to the environment

estuary (ES-choo-er-ee) an arm of the sea that meets the mouth of a river

glaciers (GLAY-shurz) slow-moving masses of ice found in mountain valleys or polar regions

habitats (HAB-uh-tats) places where an animal or a plant naturally lives

mollusks (MAH-luhsks) animals with a soft body, no spine, and usually a hard shell that live in water or a damp habitat

mudflats (MUHD-flatz) muddy wetlands that are alternately covered and uncovered by seawater

recreational (rek-ree-AY-shuhn-uhl) involving games, sports, and hobbies that people like to do in their spare time

runoff (RUN-off) rainfall that is not absorbed by the soil and eventually reaches streams and rivers

shellfish (SHEL-fish) a creature with a shell that lives in water, such as a crab, oyster, or marine mussel

strait (STRAYT) a narrow strip of water that connects two larger bodies of water

FOR MORE INFORMATION

BOOKS

Simon, Charnan, and Ariel Kazunas. *Killer Whales*. New York: Children's Press, 2013.

Tieck, Sarah. *Washington*. Minneapolis: ABDO Publishing Company, 2013.

WEB SITES

National Wildlife Federation—Wild Places: Puget Sound
www.nwf.org/Wildlife/Wild-Places/Puget-Sound.aspx
This Web site includes additional information about plants and animals found throughout the Puget Sound region.

Puget Sound Starts Here
http://pugetsoundstartshere.org
This site features fast facts about Puget Sound, as well as an online quiz and several conservation tips.

ABOUT THE AUTHOR
Katie Marsico has written more than 100 books for young readers. She hopes to one day go on a whale-watching cruise in Puget Sound.